FOREWORD BY TAMMY KLING

BEYOND 20/20 VISION

9 LIFE LESSONS
TO HELP YOU
ACHIEVE CLARITY,
TO LIVE YOUR
BEST LIFE!

DR. SUSAN TRUONG

SIGHT IS A FUNCTION OF YOUR EYES. VISION IS A FUNCTION OF YOUR HEART.

BEYOND 20/20 VISION

9
LIFE LESSONS
TO HELP YOU
ACHIEVE CLARITY,
TO LIVE YOUR
BEST LIFE!

DR. SUSAN TRUONG

SIGHT IS A FUNCTION OF YOUR EYES. VISION IS A FUNCTION OF YOUR HEART.

BEYOND 20/20 VISION
9 Life lessons to help you achieve clarity, to live your best life!
© 2021 by Dr. Susan Truong. All rights reserved.
No part of this book may be reproduced
or transmitted in any form or by any
means, electronic or mechanical, including
photocopying, recording or by any
information storage and retrieval system,
without permission in writing
from the copyright owner.

Published by Clovercroft Publishing,
Franklin, Tennessee
Edited by OnFire Books
Cover and Interior Design by
Debbie Manning Sheppard
Printed in the United States of America.
978-1-950892-72-3

DEDICATION

In my twenty plus years as an eye doctor, I have seen too many people just merely existing and not truly living. You get only one life and it's a short one. Make it count. Make it matter. Choose to make a difference. The lessons in this book are not simply words. They are how I strive to live on a daily basis. I hope you find inspiration in my book to fully live your vision. Refuse to coast through life on autopilot. A little turbulence during your journey is not necessarily a bad thing. It makes for a great wake-up call. My parents, Mai and Long Truong, did not receive a higher formal education. Nevertheless, they gathered immense wisdom from life that laid the foundation for who I am today and my core values. Their life's lessons gave me the tools and strength to better manage and cope with my own challenges.

My brother, Devon, passed away too soon but taught me so much. He reminded me that life is not measured by the number of breaths we take, but by the moments that take our breath away.

Last but not least, I am grateful to have the unending support of my husband, Steven Jeffrey, who constantly challenges me to live my own vision. He frequently reminds me that quitting is not an option.

I will love all of you always.

CONTENTS

BEYOND20/20VISION

FOREWORD

What's your vision for the future?

When I first began talking to Susan about her purpose in this world, I saw a diamond in the rough, a true teacher who bloomed anywhere she was planted. After more than two decades of seeing patients, she described to me how important each one was to her and how she had come to be so invested in their lives. Susan has been more than just Dr. Truong to her patients. She has been a solid, consistent, confident, and trusted advisor over the course of her career.

In addition to this knowledge that she had counseled and breathed life into many families, I also knew that she had reached another level: a pinnacle of growth from where it was now time to scale bigger heights. She accepted that challenge with ease. She not only bloomed where she was planted, but she continued to venture out on stage after stage, and article after article, and podcasts and coaching. I invited her to speak on our TEDx stage, addressing world changers, because Susan is a world changer herself.

Susan Truong's legacy reminds me to tell you that you can become a world changer too. The only difference is a choice. You have to make the choice to keep on moving, follow your vision, and execute the steps that will lead to it. Vision alone is not enough. You must be absolutely committed to making a commitment to achieve your dreams. Thinking about it isn't enough. As Susan would say, wake up! Do not miss this opportunity to be the best you can be.

And a word from me to you. Whatever your dream is, you can achieve it with hard work and the right mindset. But your legacy isn't about a resume or a college degree or what your parents' expectations were. My job is to equip leaders, to bring their message to the world. We do this in a myriad of ways and it always amazes me to sit with CEOs of multimillion dollar companies who still don't feel as if they are living their purpose. But purpose isn't tied to wealth or achievement. Your purpose is your calling here on earth.

Your legacy is not what you do but who you are.

Susan went to school to be a doctor, but that's the least of her achievements. Who she is inside is worth more than diamonds or rubies. She's not just a diamond in the rough. She is one of those rare people in this world who can breathe life into others and give them a word of inspiration that will change the trajectory of their own existence in life.

May her story inspire you to be the very best you can be!

Tammy Kling

TAMMY KLING
CEO, Founder, Worldschool

ACKNOWLEDGMENTS

I t is essential that I acknowledge some individuals who played vital roles in this venture and in my life.

Tammy Kling, Patti Lusk, Tiarra Tompkins, and Larry Carpenter, all of you have been there for me from day one. Thank you for your encouragement and guidance.

Larry Carpenter, I appreciate you for lighting a fire underneath my rear to keep me on track, on my timeline, and always heading toward the finish line.

Tammy Kling, thank you for always being there for me to bounce off thoughts and ideas no matter what hours of the day or night. Your tireless coaching kept me on my toes.

Patti Lusk, the cheerleader in you really made the editing process a bit more bearable. Thank you for frequently cheering me on.

Debbie Manning Sheppard, thank you for your patience through my numerous requests for changes to my cover and interior design. I love the end result!

Harold Jeffrey, thank you for being such a kind and thoughtful father-in-law. Here you are nearing 90 years of age, yet you choose to keep up with your continuing education so that you can maintain your CPA license. You inspire all of us every day just by being who you are. Thank you for always being so willing to share your life's stories and experiences, some of which I've incorporated in my book.

Linda Tuminelli, I couldn't have asked for a more thoughtful and loving girlfriend. We've been through so much together. All of which to strengthen our friendship. Thank you for always being there for me, whether as a shoulder to lean on, to lend an ear, or both. We impact others with our stories. I cherish you, my dear friend.

To all the people who have come into my life for a reason or a season, thank you for enriching my life. Whether our encounters ended positively or negatively, I gained some invaluable insights and lessons. Because of you, I am more confident, stronger, and wiser. Thank you for unknowingly contributing to my betterment.

INTRODUCTION

Change is daunting. But change is growth. Change is life. Life is change. Change is the only one constant in our lives. Change is taking place around you. Change is taking place inside you.

Often, we fear the unknown for unknown reasons. But if we continue to fear it, we get stuck and delay the greater reward.

Change is often the difference maker. It determines whether we stay in a rut or whether we pursue success.

I truly believe that if you don't change, then you will die. Change means being able to adapt and flex to the current of life. To resist change is futile. The sooner you embrace change, the easier and more peaceful your life will be.

What kind of changes have you made in your life? In my twenty years as an eye doctor, I have witnessed a myriad of changes taking place in my patients' lives. These changes occur in the areas of health, relationships, spiritual leanings, business, and finance. The only thing inevitable is change!

Undoubtedly, action, change, and success are our own choice and individual responsibility. If you want to move out of a place of complacency and into success, you have to ask yourself, how hungry am I? What can I do to change the direction that I am going? I've seen humans stuck in a bad situation for any length of time. It has been because they didn't want to change. Maybe they had a fear of the unknown, or a fear about the opportunity in front of them. But successful people eventually understand how to embrace and adapt to change. Here's the question that you need to ask yourself. Do I choose to live in faith or in fear? The answer should be very obvious.

If you have that mindset and that focus, anything is possible.

You take action. You take responsibility.

It isn't your parents' responsibility, nor your spouse's,

nor anyone else's responsibility, for that matter. Make the decision to be the CEO of your life! Take charge and determine your own destiny! Because, if you don't, somebody or something else will determine it for you. If you can take action, then you can do it. It's all up to you. You choose.

When I thought about my future, I knew that if I was going to fail or succeed, it was all on me. I didn't start this life off as an incredible success. I started at the bottom. But I knew that it was me who could make the choice to stay at the bottom or pursue my greater purpose.

In Vietnam, we were a family that could be considered wealthy. Yet everything changed suddenly, in unexpected ways. In April 1975, when South Vietnam fell into Communist rule, my parents packed up the five children and left everything that we had to start a new life in America. They wanted a better life for us, and they didn't wait for things to change around them. They took action and brought us to the United States to start over. They wanted to provide us with a better opportunity to thrive and be successful. Other families that came over at the same time would talk about the wealth they had back in Vietnam, and my father would remind them: "That doesn't matter here. We are all having to start over at the bottom."

My father was a master tailor and watching him and my mother work hard to provide for us was its own kind of training. Seeing their dedication and their commitment to success motivated me to work hard to get an education and create a life that they would be proud of. Through hard work and discipline, I became an optometrist, an international speaker, and a life coach. I've evolved as the years have gone by and so can you!

Each one of us has been bestowed with specific gifts that can change the world, if we choose to be aware of them and use them. You don't have to be Mother Theresa to make a difference and make an impact on a daily basis. You can simply start with a sincere and genuine smile.

Being an optometrist has been a blessing because not only do I literally help my patients to see, but I have the opportunity to inspire them to live their vision. Sight is a function of your eyes. Vision is a function of your heart. If you can realize that you are the determining factor for change in your life, then you can change the trajectory of your life from who you are to who you can be.

You want to know the secret sauce to being successful? It's called hunger, grit, determination, perseverance, focus, and hard work.

Your mind is the most valuable and powerful tool that

you possess. Success starts by having a positive mind-set. There are two factors that set us up for failure. First is that our mind defaults to negative thinking. And second, for some of us, our childhood was less than ideal which may lead us to live a life where we don't think that we are deserving of the best or are capable of achieving our dreams.

If you are not happy with something in your life, you have to change the way you think. That is your first step. Think different to live different. Next, it's time to create abundance in your life.

Medical studies indicate that the way you think and eat affects the way your brain works and your immune system responds. With your thinking, you can will your body into better health or lead it into illness. Eating is the same way. You can eat yourself into better health or you can eat yourself into illness. As they say, "You are what you eat." This is very true. When you eat a lighter and healthier meal, you still feel energetic when you're done eating. Eat a heavier meal, you'll feel heavy, sleepy, and sluggish afterward. Pay attention to how you feel after each meal from now on. It all comes down to the choices you make. Remember that excellent health starts from the inside out.

If you want anything badly enough, you can make it happen. It starts with your why. Your why must make you cry or it's not your why. Then you need to go find another why. Instead of making excuses, make a commitment. Make the commitment to the one big thing you want, today. Clear the clutter. As you read this book, hopefully you can make a positive change in your life. I am here for you!

We know it is easier to make excuses than to make a commitment. But if you can create a goal, make a commitment, and believe in those commitments more than anything that you ever have believed in your whole life, then you will triumph. It doesn't have to be hard, just take baby steps. Your thinking will change when you start being intentional about your choices.

Commit, Believe, Triumph

It all comes down to mindset and discipline. You have to make the decision and have the courage to make that change. I am going to show you how those small steps, those mindset changes, will help to propel you into greater success and purpose in your life. It will change your overall health and every aspect of your life. It is all tied together. The way you think determines your destiny in life, work, and love. Change the way you think so that you can start living and experiencing the best version of you. It all starts with you.

LESSON
1

Live with Intention

If you desire to live a life filled with meaning and purpose, you must be intentional with your choices. But what does it mean to live an intentional life? It means you actively engage with your life. It means you make decisions and choose your words thoughtfully and purposefully, based on what you consider to be fulfilling and meaningful to you.

Fear could get in the way and prevent you from making choices that align with your purpose. It could be fear of other people's opinions, especially those close to you, or fear of uncertainty. Fear can even disguise itself as pragmatism, forcing you to make choices that keep you comfortable, rather than putting you in a place of growth and expansion. Comfort can lead to stagnation and eventually to the death of your dreams. Fear is the enemy of intention and it will result in a lack of movement or action. As in the case of water, your purpose will remain pure and alive only when it is flowing and gaining momentum. Remove the dam of fear to keep your intention pure and alive. The life you are living today could be richer and more abundant and fulfilling, but a certain level of self-awareness is necessary for you to reach the next level. This is the first step. You must be able to take an honest look at yourself and determine whether your mindset is in harmony with your intended life or whether you're living on autopilot. Are you making intentional choices that support your purpose, or are your decisions based on fear? The heaviest burden is the thoughts in your head.

YOU CAN JUMPSTART THE PROCESS BY ASKING YOURSELF THESE QUESTIONS.

- *What does my ideal life, my dream life look like?*

_____

_____

_____

_____

_____

_____

_____

Where am I living? _____

_____

_____

_____

_____

_____

_____

Who am I with? _____

_____

_____

_____

_____

_____

_____

What am I doing? _____

_____

_____

_____

_____

_____

_____

- *Do I love my career? Why or why not?* _____

_____

_____

_____

_____

_____

_____

_____

- *Am I happy with the direction my life is going? Why or
  why not?* _____

_____

_____

_____

_____

_____

_____

_____

- *What is most meaningful to me, and how large a role does it play in my life?* _____

_____

_____

_____

_____

_____

_____

_____

_____

- *Why haven't I started the business I have been dreaming about?* _____

_____

_____

_____

_____

_____

_____

_____

_____

Questions such as these can take you a long way toward becoming aware of the choices you're making. So many things can influence the way you make decisions. Past trauma, pain, and negative experiences can come back years later and manifest as fears and insecurities.

Are your choices taking you toward being fulfilled, or are they fear-based and causing your life to stagnate?

HINT: If the first thing that crosses your mind is all the bad things that could happen if you make a decision, then you are making that decision based on fear.

Is there an area of your life where you haven't moved forward? It may be your business, your relationship with your spouse, or friction with a family member. It could even be a dream you hold dear. If so, ask yourself if there's a chance that you've allowed fear to dominate that area of your life. Fear is paralyzing, but after you have identified it, you can then work to root it out of your life for good. Once you've done that, you're on your way to living an intentional life, a life with a greater purpose.

EXERCISE
1

Here's an exercise in visualization. A powerful method to bring positive outcomes into your life!

Close your eyes and imagine what your life would be like if money is not an object.

* *Where are you living?* _____

_____

_____

_____

_____

_____

- *How are you living?* _____

_____

_____

_____

_____

_____

_____

_____

_____

- *Who's in your life?* _____

_____

_____

_____

_____

_____

_____

_____

_____

I want you to smell, feel, and taste that holiday meal that you're cooking as you are listening to the joy and laughter of the family members and friends who have gathered in your dream home.

I want you to experience this in 3D and stereo as if you're in the IMAX theater.

NOW ANSWER THE ABOVE QUESTIONS AND THE ONES IN LESSON 1.

After you're done with that, answer the final questions of this exercise:

- *What will it mean to you and your loved ones if you decide not to win?* _____

_____

_____

_____

_____

- *If you decide to give up?* _____

_____

_____

_____

_____

_____

- *To just live a life of mediocrity instead of one with intention?* _____

_____

_____

_____

_____

_____

_____

_____

_____

_____

_____

_____

- *What will that life look like?*_____

_____

_____

_____

_____

_____

_____

_____

_____

_____

_____

_____

_____

_____

_____

_____

_____

LESSON
2

Believe in Yourself

What does it mean to believe in yourself? You've heard the phrase countless times, but understanding its meaning is crucial. Many believe it simply means having self-confidence and that's definitely part of it, but there's more. It also means knowing that you, along with your ideas and dreams, are worthy of respect and acknowledgment.

When you believe in yourself, doubt will lose its power, and intentional choices become easier to make. This is what makes it possible to bring the vision for your life into reality.

Life will throw you curveballs and you will have to deal with the consequences. But no one said that you have to catch all of life's curveballs. This goes back to you having the ability to choose. The actions of others, or experiencing loss, cannot be avoided, but your belief in yourself will carry you through any of life's storms.

When you have confidence in your abilities and accept the fact that circumstances do not dictate your outcomes, you will get the courage to make intentional decisions. While others may hesitate, you boldly move forward. Everyone experiences ups and downs, but when you believe in yourself, you can stay focused, be on track, and face it all.

- *What is it that you believe about yourself?* _____

_____

_____

_____

_____

_____

_____

_____

- *List your strong attributes.* _____

_____

_____

_____

_____

Some of our patterns are manifested from the sub-conscious of our childhood. Maybe you were bullied or sexually abused. Or maybe it's just that you weren't popular, and you don't believe in yourself now. Even celebrities suffer with insecurity. There was a great movie made about the life of Elton John, his incredible musical talent, and all of the things that he had to do to get to where he is today. There was a scene in the movie where he was sitting in a therapy circle with strangers. Here, he decided to face his inner child, and at one point, he stood up and hugged him, a little boy, who represented little Elton, that young boy who'd been emotionally neglected by his father.

At some point, we have to address our inner child and adult to have a complete awareness of the things that hold us back. Maybe you feel unloved, or angry. It's time to let go! It's time to get rid of resentment or any toxicity that doesn't serve the new you!

It doesn't matter if anyone else believes in you or if you grew up poor or whatever else excuse you may have used up until now. If you were sitting in front of me, I would tell you to stop making excuses! Today is the day to leverage that small kernel of belief that you have in yourself. You know you can do a lot more than you think and you know that you can work hard to achieve your dreams.

Why do I believe in you more than you believe in yourself? Why do I see such great potential in you than you can see in yourself? It's because of your self-limiting beliefs. You limit yourself and your potential with the way you think. It doesn't matter whether I believe in you and see greater potential in you. The most important thing is that you have to believe in yourself and see greater potential in yourself.

Trust me when I tell you that life is too short not to believe in yourself. Life is too short to live mediocre. I used to be insecure in grade school and didn't believe in myself until later in life.

I will tell you how I found my vision. It was on a Tuesday late afternoon in August 2014. I was sitting in my attorney's office, which was so cold that you'd think it was an icebox when I received a call from my father. I ignored the first call since I didn't want to seem rude if I was to answer my cell phone in the middle of a meeting with my attorney. But my father was persistent. He called me again and again. Therefore, I knew that whatever he had to share with me was pretty damn serious. So, I asked for a moment to step out to take my father's call. That's when he told me that my second brother, Devon, was just diagnosed with stage 4 liver cancer.

My heart dropped to the ground and I nearly collapse on the dark grey carpet that lined the hallway of the attorney's office. All I wanted to do was to bawl my eyes out, but I couldn't and didn't do that because I knew that I had to hold my composure to return to my attorney's office to finish up our business, which I did.

After I left the attorney's office, I called my brother and he confirmed the news of his stage 4 cancer. Although our conversation was somewhat solemn, he was in good spirits. Unfortunately, his condition went downhill really fast. Nine days after that phone call, my brother Devon passed away.

His untimely death at the young age of 42 was the ultimate turning point in my life. I thought I was already living a blessed and fulfilling life. I had a highly successful career as an eye doctor operating multiple practices. But the universe had a bigger plan for me. Losing my brother had me realize that I have to serve and impact more lives beyond my small windowless dimly lit exam room. My story was too big to play small. Losing my little brother so quickly woke me up to the fact of how short and fragile life is. After his death, I decided to dedicate my life to inspiring others to live beyond the 20/20 vision. The reason why I was telling you that story is because I want you to think about that moment in your life that you may find to be your ultimate turning point. Too many of us live life as a routine. We're living on autopilot.

WAKE UP!

Be intentional and aware of your surroundings.
Spend more time with your loved ones.
Don't wait!

"MOST PEOPLE FAIL NOT
BECAUSE OF A LACK OF DESIRE
BUT BECAUSE OF
A LACK OF COMMITMENT."

VINCE LOMBARDI

"WHAT THE MIND OF MAN
CAN CONCEIVE AND BELIEVE,
IT CAN ACHIEVE."

NAPOLEON HILL

EXERCISE
2

**What will it take for you
to believe in yourself?**

_____

_____

_____

_____

_____

_____

"COMMITMENT IS
THE ULTIMATE ASSERTION
OF HUMAN FREEDOM.
IT RELEASES ALL THE ENERGY
YOU POSSESS AND ENABLES YOU
TO TAKE QUANTUM LEAPS IN
CREATIVITY."

DEEPAK CHOPRA

LESSON
3

Commit to Your Goals

What does the word commit mean to you?

Philosophers, poets, and leaders have talked about commitment in terms of giving yourself to something. Deepak Chopra talks about your life's work and how you commit to what you do in life.

When I coach others, I always talk about three powerful words: commit, believe, and triumph. All of these words are impactful, but I feel that commitment is the root of all success. If you are unwilling to commit yourself to anything, you become like a ship without a rudder, wandering with no clear direction. You're just meandering through life on autopilot.

You're merely existing and not truly living. When you are committed to your vision, you will take the necessary actions to turn your vision into reality. No matter what path you have chosen in life, the commitment must be an integral part of who you are. It's not just a word. It's an act. It transforms the promise into reality. Without commitment, you cannot have depth in anything whether it's a relationship, business, or hobby.

It's a pledge, a promise that when you start something, you'll finish it. You won't waive your commitment under any circumstances until you reach your goal because your future and the lives of others depend on you doing so. It's a willingness to give your time and energy to something that you believe in, like a person or a cause. When you are committed, you won't allow discouragement to drag you down, and you will not give up. You have more confidence to get through life's challenges, knowing that success is only a matter of time.

As a doctor, I educate my patients on the importance of improving their overall health and lifestyle by losing weight, quitting smoking, drinking moderately, exercising more, and eating healthier. The most common response I get to that advice is how difficult it is to follow. There are a million excuses to justify not doing something instead of making just one commitment to do it. Whether it's hard or not is up to you, and so is the value you place on it. If you were diagnosed with a terminal illness today and told that you had only three months left to live, would you live differently? If your answer is yes, then why wait? You can decide to change today, right this moment. There's no need to wait for something catastrophic to happen to push you into making that decision. When is the best time to start living your vision? Right here, right now!

You are not promised tomorrow.

When you're committed, you accept no excuses, only results. Committing to what you do, whether in your personal or professional life, is one of the fundamental principles of success. Commitments are powerful because they influence how you think, what you speak, how you act, and what you do. Unlike a halfhearted hope or "best shot," committing means that you work harder, you look for solutions when faced with obstacles, and quitting isn't an option.

When I left my family and hometown for optometry school to work on my doctorate (which was a full-time job), I was engaged, and my fiancé went with me. That turned out to be one of the biggest mistakes of my life, but also a huge blessing! He promised me that he would take care of me by working full time and managing all of our financial obligations. My only job was to focus on my studies, and he would tend to the rest. As it turned out, those were hollow words. He couldn't find work to save his life, and in fact, it appeared as though he wasn't trying all that hard. I would arrive home after a long day at school to find him engrossed in video games. I was engaged to a boy, not a real man!

That's pretty much how it went for my first semester of graduate school. By the second semester, I was consumed with school during the week and an 8-hour work shift on Saturdays and Sundays until I graduated four years later. Needless to say, our engagement didn't last. It took me nearly a year before I gathered up enough courage to kick him out of my life. Why? Because I was insecure. At that time, I thought my life held no meaning unless I had a man in it. Boy, was I wrong!

Our final year together was tumultuous as the fights became more volatile. I endured verbal, emotional, and physical abuse. That was my fault because I allowed it to occur. The final straw was when he choked me and nearly threw me down the stairs. I fought back, only to be restrained with duct tape. Then, he drew a loaded gun and held it to my right temple. With my adrenaline flowing, I shouted at him to pull the trigger, but he didn't have the guts to do it, for which I am now thankful. I also shouted at him that if he did pull the trigger on me, then he'd have to turn around and immediately pull it on himself. If not, my father and four brothers would hunt him down like rabid dogs and they wouldn't quit until they found him. To this day, I can still feel the cold of the gunmetal on my temple.

All of this took place while I continued to focus on my studies and keep my grades up. Those who knew me, my family, friends, professors, and classmates couldn't believe how I was able to manage this period of madness in my life and not allow it to disrupt my doctorate program. I could have chosen to be weak and let all of this craziness consume me and fail out of the program, but I didn't do that. Do you know what kept me going and prevented me from failing and getting kicked out of the program? It was the commitment I made to myself, my family, and my future. As immigrants, my parents had sacrificed so much for me to have a better opportunity than they had and to receive a higher education. Plus, I worked too hard academically in order to gain acceptance into the program that I was not about to let some narcissistic guy screw up my future. Come hell or high water, I was determined to graduate in four years with my Doctor of Optometry degree. And I did!

One of the most distinguishing characteristics of success is commitment.

The temptation to quit will arise. The key is to anticipate it and promise yourself that no matter how tempting it may get, you will never give up on your commitment.

EXERCISE
3

What are you so committed to change in your life that no one or nothing can make you waive from it because your future, your life, your loved ones depend on it?

_____

_____

_____

_____

_____

BEYOND20/20VISION

Who loses if you decide not to win? _____

_____

_____

_____

_____

_____

_____

_____

_____

_____

_____

_____

_____

_____

_____

_____

_____

_____

_____

_____

_____

_____

_____

_____

_____

_____

_____

LESSON
4

Embrace Change

Sometimes you just need a life makeover, and maybe you don't even realize it. I remember one of my patients, a Caucasian woman in her early 60s with a beautiful spirit, who came to me because she was interested in wearing contact lenses again. She had been wearing bifocal glasses and was ready for a change, a new look. She was starting her life makeover, her self-care, with me first, her eye doctor.

I learned that she had recently lost her husband and her dog.

I asked her, "You lost your husband and your dog. Now that you're alone, what is it that makes you want to get out of bed in the morning?"

She went on to tell me that she wanted to start exercising, lose weight, and simply feel better. She wanted to start her day with a high energy level.

I commended her for wanting to create a positive change and told her that it was time to focus on herself. Sometimes, all someone needs is a little positive push and encouragement from someone who genuinely cares.

Many people go through life without actually living it. Stuck on autopilot, they go through the motions without giving a thought about how to make life more meaningful. They are just merely existing and not truly living. Their life lacks vision and passion. They have become complacent and have chosen a life of mediocrity.

Life will throw you curveballs and you have to learn to deal with it. Things will happen that you can't control, but that doesn't mean you have to lose yourself in the midst of the storm.

You can try to play it safe, minimizing all risks in your life, but you'll rob yourself of so many amazing experiences. Life is an adventure, and while you don't have to be reckless, you can embrace the risks that come with living an abundant and fulfilling life.

Some people do everything they can to play it safe by avoiding failures, emotional letdowns, sadness, or physical pains. But where is the growth in that? Where is the fun in playing it safe? They don't want to risk anything. But what if you took a risk and received an exponential return on that risk? What if the biggest return on investment in life occurs when you step into the unknown?

Yes, it can be scary. But there are times in life when you just have to say, "Screw it. Let's do it. What have I got to lose?" That was how I felt when I went ziplining for the very first time. It was scary as hell as I was climbing to the top of the tall tower from where I was taking off! But once I did it, it was so much fun and exhilarating ziplining across this huge lake. The whole time I was thinking that if this line breaks, I would end up in the lake with the alligators! I can't wait to zipline again!

I've come to a place in my own life where I don't like to waste my most valuable commodity, my time. And neither should you.

Each morning, as soon as I open my eyes, I practice my attitude of gratitude. This is when I quickly mentally list three persons or things that I am grateful for. I also make the choice to be kind and live my truth. These practices set the tone for the rest of my day.

I love the freedom that comes with living an honest and authentic life.

That same freedom can be yours. You can make the same choice. You can wake up each day and choose to be empathetic, kind, compassionate, and happy. You can choose to conform or transform. It's up to you.

If reading this makes you feel a bit awkward or uncomfortable, maybe you need a life makeover. Maybe it's time to look in the mirror and ask yourself, the most important person in the universe, what it is that you want out of life. What kind of life do you truly want to live?

If you're not sure where to begin, start with what you do for work. Do you love what you do or is it just a J-O-B? Do you wake up in the morning energized and excited for the day ahead? If not, then you need to make a change. A large portion of your life is spent working, and if you don't love what you're doing, then your life will be miserable and wasted. Then you're not living into your greater purpose.

Now that I've assessed your professional life, let's take a look at your personal life. How are things at home? How's your relationship with your partner? Is your home your haven? Is it a place where you can't wait to get to after a long day at the office? A place where you can unwind and decompress or is it a place of chaos?

Existing is not living. Now is the time to start truly living your authentic life. It is never too late to pivot in order to live your vision!

Today is the day to define where you are, and where you want to go.

Your life doesn't have to be broken before you experience a makeover. It may be that you're simply settling for less. If you are settling in any area of your life, ask yourself why. It's all too easy to get in a rut, living on autopilot. Perhaps you've been working an unfulfilling job for decades, or maybe you became an engineer because your parents wanted you to. Maybe, up until now, you've been living your life for somebody else and you haven't dared to make a change.

Fear prevents many people from living a life of purpose and from recognizing their blind spots. However, it's not always fear that holds you back. Sometimes, it is simply routine or complacency or plain laziness. Routine, living in a rut, kills more dreams than fear. Complacency leads to comfort, and it's human nature to desire comfort because it's easy. Comfort will seduce you into settling for mediocrity instead of making a change and striving for all that life has to offer.

Your life makeover can begin today. Today is your day! All it takes is one small step. One positive change can start the process of creating a new life for yourself.

The famous life coach, Tony Robbins, teaches you to unleash the power within you. You can do this. I have done it, and so can you. I am here to hold your hand through this amazing process of self-discovery.

EXERCISE
4

Go and look in the mirror. How much do you like and love that person who is looking back at you? What do you want to change and improve about yourself? Make a list with these four headings, creating four columns:

WHAT TO CHANGE	WHY I WANT THE CHANGE	DESIRED RESULTS	HOW TO DO IT

WHAT TO CHANGE	WHY I WANT THE CHANGE	DESIRED RESULTS	HOW TO DO IT

You know that you're ready for your ultimate self-care, your ultimate makeover, but you're not sure as to how to go about it. That's where I come in as your coach. You can contact me at **Dr.Susan@beyondyour2020vision.com**

LET'S GET TO WORK!

LESSON
5

Be Mindful

There are two different ways you can approach life: with mindfulness or with mindlessness.

Mindlessness means you're going through the motions, living on autopilot without thinking of the impact your decisions have on your life.

The opposite of mindlessness is mindfulness. It is being

self-aware and conscious of your actions and the impact they have on your life. It is living life intentionally.

When you live mindfully, you make better choices. You will experience more success because you're paying attention. You know at the time of decision-making the impact that decision will have on your life. This gives you confidence in yourself and your ability to create positive change.

People often think confidence means you aren't afraid to step on stage and speak to 10,000 people. While that is partly true, being confident means so much more. When you are confident, you dare to make a decision, even when no clear answer exists. It doesn't always mean the absence of fear, but rather the strength to keep moving forward in spite of it.

Where fear will cause you to hesitate, confidence will keep you moving. Where fear is indecisive, confidence is making the call, taking action, and getting things done.

Indecisiveness and inaction can get you killed, especially while trying to navigate through heavy traffic. The sooner you can make a decision with confidence and take massive action, the sooner you will achieve success in navigating life's superhighways.

You can apply this concept to your career. If you are being hesitant and indecisive, you could be missing out on opportunities that could change your life and your trajectory toward your goals. Of course, you can apply this concept to all areas of your life, goals, dreams, and relationships. Imagine, for example, the positive changes that could occur in your close relationships if you live mindfully, being aware of how your actions are impacting others. How many misunderstandings and hurt feelings could be prevented? Think of how much richer life would be.

If you feel you lack confidence, you can change that too. Be mindful of your speech, the words you use. If you focus on why something *can't* be done, or why it's *impossible*, or *unlikely*, you will develop thought patterns that lead to indecisiveness. Conversely, if you choose to focus on why it *can* be done, or that it *will* happen, or that a solution *does* exist, you will create thought patterns that lead to a confident mindset.

You already have everything inside you that you need to accomplish your goals. There isn't a magic formula. It's all about learning your strengths and weaknesses then learning to use both as tools instead of handicaps. It's about being self-aware and recognizing when fear is becoming an obstacle. It's about intentionally developing a winning mindset.

The bottom line is this:

Fear holds you back.
Confidence moves you forward.
One is a step backward,
whereas the other,
a step forward
toward living your vision.

EXERCISE
5

Our mind defaults to negative thinking. Like the defaults on your computers and mobile phones, you have the option to change those settings. Let's reprogram your mind's defaults to positive thinking by doing this exercise:

I want you to go 24 hours straight without thinking, speaking, or doing anything negative. Your thoughts, feelings, and actions will be all positive for the next 24 hours. This exercise will transform your life! Do this for 24 hours straight, then another 24, then another 24. You get the picture. Soon, it will become second nature. A habit. A new norm. Soon, it will be the only way you know. A positive mindset. A positive life. In this new life, you will find an opportunity in every adversity.

Next, face your fears by listing them here.

_____

_____

_____

_____

_____

_____

_____

_____

_____

_____

_____

*What is holding you back
from living your vision,
from living your best life,
and from your dream life?*

LESSON
6

Eat to Live

Proper nutrition is an often overlooked topic in the lives of most people. When I coach clients, I always cover health and nutrition because its impact on the quality of life cannot be overstated. What you put into your body matters. Excellent health starts from the inside out. One of the best indications of your health is your waistline. Let me help you to better trim and maintain your ideal waistline.

I've lost count of how many times I have had someone, such as most of my patients, tell me, when I coach them on proper nutrition, that, "I'm too busy to do that" and "Eating healthy is too expensive."

At that point, I let them know that there's nothing else I can do. You have to want to be the change that you want to see. Help me to help you. At the end of the day, you have to love yourself enough to make a positive and dramatic change. As the old saying goes, "When the student is ready, the teacher will appear."

In an age where there are fast-food restaurants on every corner and mega supermarkets filled with processed foods, most people have forgotten how to fuel their bodies with proper food. Something I tell my patients and clients who I coach is to carefully consider everything you put into your mouth. Ask yourself this question each time you're about to eat or drink something: "Am I eating and drinking to live or to die?" It seems harsh, but it's the truth. You're either eating or drinking to fuel and energize this incredible vehicle known as your body, or you're killing it slowly by ingesting toxins from processed foods. Remember, you are what you eat. Garbage in equals garbage out.

I want you to enjoy eating. I love eating! I love all different types of cuisine! We have a sense of smell and taste for a reason. I don't want you to think that in order to eat healthier, you have to deprive yourself of all those guilty pleasures such as steaks, pizza, hamburgers, fries, desserts, and so on. The key is eat to live, not eat out of boredom or to comfort your emotional issues.

Another thing to consider when eating is the portion size and how you eat. Let's start with portion size. In the United States, supersizing food orders are quite common because the fast-food industry makes it so easy for the consumers. Also, the supersize is perceived as giving the best value for the money spent. At least that's what my husband, who I affectionately call my white boy, thinks. At this point, I can't help but roll my eyes at him.

The concept is not too different when it comes to eating at a buffet. You pay a nominal charge to eat at the buffet, therefore, come hell or high water, you're going to take your time and eat your money's worth, if not more. For most, this is the mindset. It gets worse the more you pay for the buffet, the longer you'll tend to sit and graze because you vowed not to miss a single item on that buffet setup! That was exactly our thinking when my family and I used to frequent local Chinese buffets on a monthly basis a few years ago. We ate as if it was going to be our last meal! We were such gluttons for punishment. And believe me, we felt like crap for many hours afterward. Now, we avoid buffets. We don't even miss them.

How much food you eat is as important as the quality of the food you eat. Eating large portions can lead to indigestion and discomfort. Your digestive system functions best when it is not overloaded with too much food. Overeating disrupts your blood sugar balance by overloading your body with glucose, which can lead to insulin resistance. This, along with a sedentary lifestyle, has caused an epidemic of type 2 diabetes in the United States. This is another case where self-awareness is crucial. Be aware and conscious about what you eat and how much you eat.

Next, let's talk about why how you eat is also important to your health and well-being. I love to watch people when I'm out and about, at stores, airports, restaurants, salons, out on the road, to name a few places. After years of observing American strangers and my friends eat, I have concluded that the majority of them gulp down their food very rapidly. It's as if it was an eating competition or they were worried that someone was going to snatch their food away at any second. Stop this, America! From now on, I want you to make love to your food when you're eating. Here's how you can do it. Eat only bite-sized pieces, enough to comfortably fit into your mouth. There is no need to gorge yourself nor store food in your cheeks, because you're not a squirrel. Chew slowly and thoroughly. Savor all the different flavors and spices that are in that one bite. This is how you make love to your food. Studies have indicated that when you eat slowly and chew thoroughly, you will tend to be more slender. Also, can you truly taste and enjoy your food when you're just gulping it down so quickly?

Remember when I said that commitment is not just a word. It's a daily act. It transforms the promise into reality. Health doesn't happen by accident. It's a daily commitment to action. Not accident, but action. What daily habits do you have that drive your health and wellness? Some people start the day with meditation, reading, motivation, music, or affirmations.

Passion fuels commitment because when you're passionate about something, you're driven to want it, get it, and sustain it. So, apply this same passion for staying healthy!

As a doctor who chooses to practice holistically, I educate my patients on the importance of improving their overall health and lifestyle by losing weight, quitting smoking, drinking moderately, exercising more, and eating healthier. Yes, I am an eye doctor, but my patients are not just a set of eyeballs sitting in my exam chair. I treat my patients as a whole person, from top to bottom, inside to out. What they eat, drink, and how well they rest and handle life's stress will impact their life. As an optometrist, I literally help my patients to see 20/20, but as a visionary strategist, I am inspiring them and you to live your vision, in this case, your vision of ideal health.

Learning to care for your health through proper nutrition and eating habits is no different than making a positive change in any other area of your life. It takes self-control and self-discipline. You have to be proactive and take the initiative. Do not wait for a wake-up call such as a heart attack, stroke, or pandemic before you decide to scrap your not-so-great current eating habits for healthier ones.

Most people think that learning to eat healthy is so complicated. It doesn't have to be. Let me give you some tips that will help make it easier for you. Start by eating more of a plant-based diet, which means more fruits and vegetables and less meat. When you go to the grocery store, shop the perimeter because that is where you will find healthier foods such as fresh fruits and vegetables, dairy products, meats, and seafood. Of course, minimize your consumption of meats and seafood. The aisles in the middle of the store contain some yummy treats, but they aren't so great for us since they are man-made and processed. That's why many of those items don't need to be refrigerated.

Four other easy tips to remember that will help you to make better and healthier choices while shopping are:

- *The faster that item will spoil when left out on the counter, the better for you. That bag of potato chips will never spoil, but watch how fast the tomatoes go!*

- *Get in the habit of reading package labels. Look at the ingredients. If an average eight-year-old child can read it, then it's good for you. If that child has difficulty reading the ingredients, then it's not so healthy for you. The reason is that better and healthier foods are made of natural ingredients, which consist of shorter words that are easier to read. The ingredients of man-made processed foods usually are comprised of long words that are hard to pronounce because they are chemicals.*

- *Read the labels again. This time, pay attention to the calories, carbohydrates, fat, sugar, and sodium. In these categories, you want to make sure that those levels are low. The more sugar and carbohydrate you eat, the more you'll crave it.*

- *And never go grocery shopping while you're hungry! You will make smarter and healthier choices when you shop with a full stomach. Your life depends on it. Love yourself enough to make any changes necessary to ensure you live the highest quality of life possible.*

EXERCISE
6

**Practice self-control and self-discipline.
Here's how:**

Go shopping with a list and stick to it!

Write down everything that you eat and drink every day! Everything that you put in your mouth!

When you see it all written down, it seems more real!

BEYOND 20/20 VISION

You are either going to be quite proud of yourself or quite disgusted. Before you put anything in your mouth, whether solids or liquids, ask yourself this question: "Am I eating to live or to die?" Sounds harsh, but it's practicing tough love for yourself and your health. Choose wisely.

LESSON
7

Think Your Way to Success

"YOU ARE WHAT YOU THINK ALL DAY LONG."

RALPH WALDO EMERSON

You have a vision of how you want your life to be. The question you have to ask yourself is, "Are my thoughts in alignment with my vision?"

Your thoughts shape your reality. If that sounds complicated or like something based on a new-age belief system, it isn't. It is based on psychology. If you think of yourself as a failure, you will feel like a failure, and then you will act like a failure. Of course, the opposite is true as well. If you think of yourself as successful, you will feel successful and like a successful person would act.

The thoughts running through your head profoundly affect your mood and state of mind. The decisions you make are fueled by your state of mind, so you can see why it is important to align your thoughts with your desired outcome.

An important distinction to make when it comes to your thoughts is whether they are based on fact or fear. While fear can be a useful emotion, left unchecked, it will dominate your thoughts and decisions. If fear is driving your thoughts, you will think of all the reasons why you can't do something rather than the reasons why you can.

If your thoughts are not in alignment with your life vision, how can you change your thoughts?

If you are already aware of the fact that your thoughts do not align with your vision, you've won half the battle. Awareness is the first step.

Once you are aware that you need to shift your thinking,

you are ready for the next step, which is your self-talk. This is a proven strategy that will transform your mindset. Begin by focusing on the language you use when talking to and about yourself. Start your day by planting positive language into your mind. How you begin your day has a powerful and long-lasting effect on the rest of your day. Use the power of gratitude and focus on at least three things for which you are grateful. This practice has been proven to induce feelings of happiness that are long-lasting.

Another useful tool is visualization. There's a reason why professional athletes use this technique. When you visualize things going the way you want and vividly picture your desired outcome, you are programming your mind to look for and identify opportunities and solutions. It's training your mind for success.

Success means different things to different people, and the worst thing you could do is define success through someone else's eyes. Stay true to your vision and achieve your success.

"WHAT THE MIND OF MAN CAN CONCEIVE AND BELIEVE, IT CAN ACHIEVE."

NAPOLEON HILL

At this very second, where is your mindset? Where has it been the last year or two? Understand that your mindset drives everything! Like the energy that surrounds us, your mindset is either positive or negative. There's no in-between. It's either seeing the glass half-full or half-empty. Your mindset, the way you think, sets the tone for your day, your life. What you think becomes your actions, which becomes your results. If you live life with a greater purpose, then that purpose will direct your life with better clarity, clarity beyond 20/20 vision.

A shift in mindset can alter the trajectory of your life by bridging the gap between who you are today and who you can be. Your mindset affects every cell in your body. Studies have revealed that a positive mindset can cure an illness, a disease, while a negative mindset can certainly kill you.

Let me share a positive mindset story with you. One of my patients, at the age of thirty-five, was diagnosed with early-stage breast cancer. She had no family history of it. The news was devastating at first, but she decided that she was not going to let this throw her into a depression. There was no plan for any treatment yet because the doctors had to conduct further testing. I've been caring for this patient for the last ten years, so I've gotten to know her quite well. Each time she comes into our office, she was always such a happy and bubbly individual. Because of her attitude of gratitude and a constant positive outlook on life, she made the decision that she was going to beat this cancer.

I often tell patients that your problems, issues, challenges, or new diagnosis do not define you. You have to take ownership, take control, and be at the helm of your life. This patient continued living with her healthy lifestyle choices: eating well, maintaining a positive mindset, and not letting stress get to her. Two months after her diagnosis, she baffled her oncologist when she returned for her follow-up visit and was cancer-free. Her doctor did not have any real scientific explanation for what happened. However, the patient attributed this miracle to her positive attitude and outlook on life. To her, the glass was always half-full.

Alternatively, here is a negative mindset story. This occurs at a personal level. It involves a very close friend of my husband. He's a nice guy, but it's never his fault. He's always the victim. It's always someone else's fault: his wife, his children, the politicians, or the economy. I truly believe that it is for this reason that he is frequently sick, whether it's a cough, cold, headache, or aches and pains somewhere on his body. It's always something. As they say, misery loves company. But, in reality, nobody loves them or wants to be near them. His wife and my husband attempted to point out his negativity to him, but in his mind, he sees nothing wrong with him. Might as well be talking to the wall. We can't help someone who thinks he is already perfect. For him, he sees his glass as half-full, when the effect he has on all those around him is one of half-empty.

After today, I want you to pay closer attention to the thoughts and self-talk that you, yourself, have every day and of those around you. The people with an incredibly positive mindset tend to be much happier and healthier. They lead a very purposeful life. They light up the room every time they walk in. Others are drawn to the immense peaceful energy that they radiate.

The people with a negative mindset will tend to be sick more frequently and look older, and darkness seems to follow them wherever they go. No one wants to be around them because of the toxic energy that they exude. It's quite sad actually that they don't realize how they are. Or how they can easily change to see the glass as half-full with one simple decision.

Let me share my own mindset story with you. When my younger brother, Devon, passed away unexpectedly, it hit me like a ton of bricks. I went through the stages of grieving. At first, it was denial then anger and then sadness. Eventually, I reached acceptance. It wasn't fair that he died at such a young age. Would I have felt better if he died at ninety-two instead of forty-two? Maybe. However, I've come to learn that your life is not necessarily defined by the length of it. Instead, it's better defined by how well and how richly you lived, by the impact and legacy that you've left behind. My brother may have had only forty-two years on this earth, but while he was here, he made every moment count. He made a difference in many lives, especially his patients'. He lived his life fully and true to himself. He played by his own set of rules. He didn't gently stroll out of this life. He skidded out of here! We should all strive to live similarly!

When he was first diagnosed, I was willing to do whatever it took for him to continue living. I was even willing to trade my life for his. Yes, I made a deal with the devil; my life for my brother's. But that wasn't in the big plan for me. The universe wasn't going to have it like that. It was simply time for my brother to go, and it wasn't my time yet. The universe had bigger plans for me.

When my brother died nine days after his diagnosis, I was so distraught that I spiraled down into the ugly dark abyss of depression. I had no desire to live anymore. I didn't want to get out of bed. I didn't want to do anything. My husband reminded me of all the reasons that I have to keep on living. But we all know that you can't lead someone out of the darkness until they are ready to receive the light of day again. After three weeks of living in this hell, I told myself that I can choose to stay in this ugly dark abyss of depression and eventually die or get out of bed and be grateful for all that I still have left, even though I just lost my little brother. He would not have tolerated me staying in that state of depression. I've come to realize that life is too short and fragile. That every day above ground is a blessing and a miracle. I chose life because many still need me and depend on me: my family, staff, and patients. They were waiting for me to get back into the game, the game of life! At that moment, I decided to turn something tragic into magic!

I shared the story with you because normally I'm a positive, happy, bubbly person, but losing my brother nearly killed me. I shared my story because I want you to know that you have the power to turn your life around. It starts with that one decision to do so. That's it. Don't make it so hard because life doesn't have to be that hard. We, as human beings, tend to complicate life way more than necessary. Learn to simplify the decision-making process in your life. You'll be so much happier.

Your mind is your greatest asset, your computer, your most powerful tool. Since you were born, it's been programmed by your parents, teachers, society, the media, and so on. There are all kinds of crazy viruses in there. But now that you are your own person and the CEO of your own destiny, get rid of those viruses and any negative programs that are slowing down your computer, your life, by rebooting it! Start today! Allow nothing in your life except positiveness! If, and when, negativeness comes along, kick it to the curb!

"HE WHO CHERISHES A BEAUTIFUL
VISION, A LOFTY IDEAL IN HIS
HEART, WILL ONE DAY REALIZE IT."

JAMES ALLEN, AUTHOR OF

AS A MAN THINKETH

EXERCISE
7

Each morning, practice what I call an attitude of gratitude. Here is what you do: as soon as you open your eyes, list three things and/or persons that you are grateful for. This truly helps to set the tone for the rest of your day.

Always think in terms of what you have instead of what you don't have. This is known as living in abundance, not scarcity. Thinking and living in this manner will consistently keep life in a positive perspective. Now make a list of your blessings, of all that you are grateful for.

BEYOND 20/20 VISION

LIST OF YOUR BLESSINGS

_____

_____

_____

_____

_____

_____

_____

_____

_____

_____

_____

_____

_____

_____

_____

_____

_____

_____

LESSON
8

Live with Passion

L ife has to have depth. It cannot be simply mediocre.

Otherwise, we'd have to continually ask ourselves: Why am I here? What am I trying to do and why do I exist on this earth? No matter what the why is, you must know that if you are going to do it, you should do it well. I know that I will always put in every effort to be all in, whatever I do.

These are the thoughts humans have when they discover a new path and a new way of living!

If not, why bother?

Passion is real. I'm not good at being fake, so I am who I am and what I do. Everyone needs to live out their authentic self and passion! I love to see people grow. When they step into their passion, it's them being their authentic self and this giant light bulb comes on.

Passion is power. It's the engine that pushes you forward and moves you toward your goals! If I'm not passionate about it, it's not a goal. It won't drive me.

One of the most powerful and useful emotions for accomplishing a goal is passion. Passion is the burning desire that keeps you moving and learning whatever is necessary to achieve your goal. If you don't have passion, then don't even begin because you will grow weary of the pursuit.

If you've gotten to the point where you dread going to work, or you've given up with trying to make your dream a reality, then the fire is gone. You're not going to see it through because you lack the passion for it.

I spent my first career in medical research. It was interesting and I learned so much in the areas of protein chemistry, molecular genetics, HIV, bone marrow transplant, collagen R&D, to name a few. However, after six years, I decided that I did not want to spend the rest of my life as a lab rat. Why? Because I had determined that I did not have a burning passion for it.

Passion comes from having a strong "why" or reason for whatever it is you're wanting to do. Your why needs to make you cry or it's not your why. Then it's time to find another why. Maybe you want to leave a legacy for your children, or perhaps you want to make a difference in the world. Whatever it is, that is where you will draw your passion.

I am passionate about impacting lives and making a difference every day. Everyone gets discouraged sometimes, but when you have a passion for life, you will find the strength to pick yourself up, dust the dirt off, and climb back on that horse. No matter what obstacle gets thrown in your path, you will find a way through, around, over, or under it.

Passion is your engine and conviction is your fuel. Passion and conviction are often viewed as synonymous, but there is a subtle distinction. Passion is an intense emotion that cannot be contained. Conviction is a firmly held belief. When you are convinced, beyond any doubt, that the work you're doing is valuable, that firmly held belief becomes the fuel that ignites your passion.

When you step into your passion, you are living your authentic self. You will work toward your goal with confidence.

Passion not only benefits you, but it benefits others as well. Passion is contagious. I've had many patients, after making their observation, who have commented on how passionate I am about being an eye doctor. After thanking them, I would reply in return that if I wasn't passionate about it, then I shouldn't be taking care of them. That I should move on and find another career. Too many people won't do that because of fear of change. They are too comfortable living a life of mediocrity. When you have passion, people see it and feel it! People can feel the real!

And they get inspired!

"WHAT WE SEE CLOUDS OUR JUDGMENT; WHAT WE DON'T SEE BIAS OUR BEHAVIORS."

AUTHOR UNKNOWN

To live best with passion and greatest clarity, you must first address your blind spots. Do you know your blind spots? It's a bit of a catch-22 because some may ask, "How would I know what my blind spots are when I can't see them?" Everybody has them, but we don't know they exist until they cause a problem. Blind spots are defined as obstacles that block the view of your dreams, your ideal lifestyle. They are your issues and negative self-talk that resulted from your past experiences. You have subconsciously accepted them as part of your life because it's easier than confronting them head on! You have become "blind" and numb to them, less aware of them. Blind spots are the result of your brain operating on autopilot. Experts tell us that the unconscious mind makes the majority of our decisions. It is imperative to identify your blind spots. Own them without being defensive and adjust behavior to compensate for them. The problem with blind spots is you don't know what you don't know.

In the back of your eyes, on your retina, you do have an actual area called the blind spot. It's called that because it doesn't receive any stimuli from the outside world due to a lack of receptors in that area. If you don't address your own blind spots, if you don't confront them yourself, then you can end up not receiving any new stimuli from the outside world. You will end up living in a world that is stale and stagnant. In order to move toward living your vision and making it a reality, you have to address your blind spots, bringing them to a resolution. If not, then they will anchor you down.

The definition of a blind spot is an area where a person's view is obstructed. This is easily observed when we're driving. As when driving, in order to get out of the blind spot, we need to continue to move forward. We need to continue driving. Same thing as in life. If our view is obstructed by our blind spot, then we move to an area where we can have a full view. Sounds simple enough, but most won't do it! If you want something bad enough, you will go over, under, around, through it — whatever it takes to move past the obstruction, the blind spot.

Let me be brave and share with you my blind spot. It consisted of work and being too ambitious. These two things obstructed my view from what was most important to me, my family. I had my head buried so deep into building my medical career and expanding to multiple practice locations that I was neglecting to spend quality time with my family, especially with my elderly parents. I'm not sure whether I see this as fortunate or unfortunate when I tell you that it took losing my little brother to snap me out of my blind spots. Yes, it's unfortunate and sad that my brother passed away. But was it a blessing in disguise because it woke me up to the fact of how short and fragile life is? I believe so. In spirit, my brother was trying to remind me of what's most important, family. At first, I was ashamed to admit this. It made me seem like a horrible daughter. That was not my intention at all. Although my parents live only

35 miles away from me, I would go for months without visiting them. How terrible was that? My parents were always so understanding, attributing it to me being so busy with work. I'm a lucky girl to have such incredible parents, but that did not excuse my behavior! Things are different now. My husband and I are now committed to working smarter and not harder. We also committed to making more time to spend with one another and with family. Now, my husband and I enjoy date night weekly and monthly getaways. I also see my parents and the rest of the family weekly now, unless I'm traveling.

I implore you to value and cherish every moment you have with your loved ones. Life can be taken away and can change within a matter of seconds, within a blink of an eye. You just never know. Being alive is such an incredible gift. Don't take it for granted. Don't let those blind spots deter you from who is most important to you.

Until you have made that decision to confront your blind spots, they will continue to haunt you. Refuse to live like that for another second! Take control by grabbing the helm of your life!

Another very important aspect of living with passion is valuing your time. Don't squander it. Don't give it out too freely. Time is our most precious commodity. Time is infinitely more precious than money. There's nothing common between them. You cannot accumulate time. You cannot borrow time. You cannot tell how much of it you have left in the bank of life. Time is life ... spend it well.

How well do you manage your time? How productive are you with your day? Some people feel like they don't have enough time in the day to accomplish things and want more hours in the day. We all have the same 24 hours in the day, but why are some of us more productive than others? Are you one to use your time wisely or do you squander it? It takes discipline and focus to have efficiency in your day. It's about prioritizing. You have to stay laser-focused on the task that's right in front of you. Minimize distractions. Don't scroll mindlessly on social media or waste time watching trash television unless that was a dedicated time for you to relax your brain and intentionally watch mindless television. I have no judgment about that decision. But worry less about what's going on to the right or left of you. Have an agenda that you must adhere to!

People say they're busy. Busy doing what? Is it a purposeful busy? Or is it busy just to be busy? Busy people actually don't have time to announce that they are busy. They put their heads down and do the work without having to broadcast it.

As we exist on this earth, it's a constant battle between the forces of good and evil. On the topic of time, good equals productivity. Evil would be defined as distractions, temptations, and procrastination. Don't let the devil win. Good will always prevail.

In *Outwitting the Devil*, written by Napoleon Hill, the author is interviewing the Devil. Hill stated that time is a friend of the person who trains his mind to follow positive-thought habits and the enemy of the person who drifts into negative-thought habits. The Devil will also tell you that he can easily control 98 percent of the people's minds. They're called drifters because their mind easily drifts. They get off task, lose focus, and get distracted easily. These days, we call that attention deficit disorder and it's "fixed" with a pill!

Breaking down the 24 hours, in general, you have 8 for sleeping, 8 for working, and the other 8 for investing in yourself. Starting this moment, with anything that you spend time on, ask yourself this question: Is this moving me closer to my ultimate goal? That may be starting up a new business, achieving a healthier lifestyle, studying for an important exam, or having more free time with family. Whatever your ultimate goal is, the purpose behind it should always be the driving factor for you to best maximize your time.

In today's world, where we have technology at our fingertips, it's easy to get distracted and off course. But I have so much that I want to accomplish in my day that I have to stay focused and eliminate distractions, such as social media.

I'm going to share something with you that I'm a bit ashamed of and embarrassed about. I have a crazy obsessive compulsive disorder (OCD), where whatever I'm doing, I feel the need to do it at least three times, if not more. Some examples: turning off lights, closing and locking doors, closing drawers, putting on my sunglasses, putting my credit cards away in my wallet. I can go on, but no need for that. You get the picture. My OCD is not bad enough where they have to lock me up in a padded room. Not all of my OCDs are a time waster. Some actually drive me to be very organized both at home and work. Every second and minute spent on repeating my tasks are an absolute waste of my valuable time. I've modified my behavior so that I can regain my time. Nonproductive things that you do, which only take a few minutes here, a few minutes there, those few minutes add up to a lot of wasted time in a 24-hour period.

People will say that they didn't realize how much time they spent on Facebook or playing video games. I'm not buying it. How can you not be aware of how much time had passed? Were you that hypnotized by it? The time is displayed all around you. You have it on your cell phone screen, your watch, the clock in your car when you're driving, and the clocks around the house. Excuses don't excuse you!

To get more accomplished, you need to have discipline, focus, and an organizer/calendar system. There are many tools out there that can help you with this.

Highly successful people are very organized, detail-oriented, fast thinkers, list makers, and live on a calendar! They place a very high value on their time. Every second matters and is accounted for. They have a system in place that helps to increase the efficiency in their day. It's seldom that they forget what they're supposed to do or phone calls that need to be made. It's often said that if you want to become more successful, then learn and emulate the best. But as a reward, they allow themselves quality time with loved ones. Work hard, play hard. That's what I always say.

Today's smartphones have many tools and apps that can keep you on task and on schedule. Take advantage of this convenient technology that's right there in your hand. Use the calendar scheduler, set up reminders, and take notes.

HERE ARE SOME TIPS TO HELP MAXIMIZE YOUR TIME AND PRODUCTIVITY:

1. *Start your day with a list of things that you tend to waste time on.*

2. *Set daily goals with reminders. (Some management apps: Timely, Trello, and Workflow).*

3. Complete the most important task first.

4. Stop multitasking. Focus on one task at a time. Whatever you're doing, give it your 100 percent.

5. Make use of dead time. Some examples of dead time are waiting at the doctor's office, the airport, and the bank. Take advantage and be productive with your dead time.

6. Read time management books (and take advice and action)!

   Some books: *Getting Things Done* by David Allen, *Eat That Frog* by Brian Tracy, and *The 4-Hour Workweek* by Tim Ferriss

Now stop wasting time! Get moving to achieve your ultimate goal, your ideal lifestyle!

Seek and maintain clarity

At this point in your journey, you've probably achieved clarity and understanding of many things. Now is the time to take action. As you continue on your life's journey to be the best that you can be and live out your purpose, you will need to maintain clarity.

How will you now maintain the clarity that you've obtained? Easier said than done. It's the same as at the beginning of each year, people make new year resolutions to lose weight, work out more, and be healthier. You know those people. It's great and exciting for a while, then the excitement fizzles out and you regress back to your old habits and routine.

Here's one method of maintaining your clarity. Ask yourself: What's at stake if you don't maintain this clarity, this new way of life? I guarantee you that once you incorporate this into your daily life, you'll see and reap the benefits of it at home, at work, and everywhere you go. You won't want to go back to your previous life because that life may have been too dark, painful, toxic — filled with negative energy.

Now that you have a clear and concise vision, one that is beyond 20/20 and living a happier and healthier life, a more abundant and fulfilling life, there's no reason to put your life in reverse. There's no turning back after this. It's all about moving forward now.

Think about when we're driving. We spend the majority of our time focusing forward at what's ahead and less time looking in the rearview mirror at what's behind us. You can use this analogy in life. The past is the past. You can look back at it occasionally, but every day is a new day, a new life, a new you dawning. Every day is a brand-new chance to move forward.

Here's how I maintain my clarity. I am consistent. I am consistent with my words, my behavior, my daily routine, and my diet. Consistency is the key in all aspects of our lives. I always keep in mind my purpose and why I work so hard every day the way I do. I do it for my family. I also want to build a legacy that I can leave behind for many generations to come. I drive myself hard every day because I'm passionate about making a difference. If I can impact just one soul per day, that's 365 souls per year times 10 years, 20 years, and so on. You get the picture. I practice discipline because it plays a critical role in helping me to attain my desired goals. I don't believe in multitasking. It does not work that well because you're not as efficient nor productive. It's better to be laser-focused on just one task at a time. I utilize all of these attributes to operate my life at home and work.

Practice everything that you've learned in these lessons every day. Live it, and it will become second nature, and you won't even have to think about it.

Once you begin to live this new way of life, your family and friends will notice a change in you. They will like what they're seeing and want to be more like you!

EXERCISE
8

ANSWER THESE QUESTIONS TO HELP CLARIFY YOUR PASSION:

What is your why? _____

_____

_____

Your why needs to make you cry or it's not your why.

Why do you do what you do even when you don't feel like it? _____

_____

BEYOND20/20VISION

What are you passionate about? _____

_____

_____

_____

_____

Who and what sets your heart and soul on fire and why? _____

_____

_____

Who and what occupies your thoughts during many of your waking hours and why? _____

_____

_____

_____

_____

_____

_____

Let's do another exercise. I'm going to share some tips with you on how to eliminate your blind spots. Let's imagine going to an Alcoholics Anonymous meeting. The first step is to admit that you have a problem. To own that problem. Then you stand in front of the group to announce your admission. Now the healing process can begin. This is how I see it with blind spots. First, you have to recognize your blind spots. What are they? How are they hindering your life, hindering you from moving forward? You have got to own your blind spots!! Now write down three of your blind spots. When things are written down and in front of your face, it makes it more real! Now you can see it for what it is. Can you accept it for what it is? Don't be ashamed of them or embarrassed by them any longer. Let it go! Set it free! Make a decision to not be a prisoner to your blind spots for another second. Now that you've done all the steps, don't you feel better and lighter? Do you feel more free? See how it is so much easier now to move forward with your vision, your dreams, your life?

How clear is your vision? How focused are you? Manifest your vision and clarity by making a vision board. Whatever you want in your life, get it on this board! This will help you to gain the best clarity and achieve your dreams more easily because you'll see it every day. Vision boards serve as extraordinary reminders!

_____

_____

_____

_____

_____

_____

_____

_____

LESSON
9

Be You

You have more power than you realize. You have the power to change your own life and the power to influence those around you. When you are committed to the outcome, you will become a positive force for good in the world. Remember, commitment implies action and it will transform the promise into reality.

When you are committed, you have a strong intent and

focus toward the things you want to accomplish. This passionate dedication is the source of your power and is what attracts people to you. When people become attracted to you, it's because they can see your light shining brightly, and like the proverbial moth to the flame, they are drawn to you. Besides people looking for help or guidance, you will also attract people into your inner circle and your tribe and also people who will compliment and support your life mission.

Everyone needs a life partner or people who support their dreams. It may be your spouse, friend, or someone who lets you know how magnificent you are! I am blessed to have found mine in my husband. Some people find their friends in group activities or hobbies. Socialization is one of the most important aspects of a healthy life.

As an optometrist, I help my patients to gain and maintain their best sight and eye health. As a life coach, I guide and inspire you to live your vision. Sight is a function of your eyes. Vision is a function of your heart. You have the best clarity of your vision, dream life, and goals when your eyes are closed and your mind and heart are opened.

I choose to be more than an eye doctor to my patients. I am also their life coach if and when the situation seems fitting. I coach my patients on nutrition, health and wellness, mindset, relationships, overcoming their fears, minimizing anxiety, how to continue living after losing a loved one, whatever topics that come up in the flow of our conversation. I coach on what it means and takes to live your vision. To live the life that you are meant to live. The life that you are deserving of.

Consider the people you come into contact with every day. How can you add light to their lives?

I think you will agree that the world needs us to shine our light. The more ways you can find through which to lift up or support another person, the more you will impact the world for good.

You have no idea how small acts of kindness can really turn someone's day around. It is the little thing that counts the most.

Need some ideas on how to shine your light?

SOME EXAMPLES OF HOW I LOVE TO BRIGHTEN SOMEONE'S DAY:

1. Pay someone a compliment.

2. Hold the door open for someone.

3. Buy coffee/tea or pay for the groceries or toll for the person behind you.

4. Give a genuine smile.

5. Let someone know that you're thinking of them.

So simple and quick, yet so effective.

What are some small acts of kindness that you love doing? What are your favorite ways to give to others?

Giving doesn't just benefit others; it takes you out of your own self-reflection. Have you ever known someone who was so into their own journey that they never seemed to focus on others? Always thinking of which direction is best for themselves and self-analyzing continually? Those people can become lifelong seekers, driven by the constant seeking, not the connecting—boring nomads, wandering the earth. It's fine to wander but at some point, why not become the giant, solid tree that has put down roots?

Why not be the tree?

PLEASE ASK YOURSELF:

How can I give more without just living in a perpetual state of existence? Don't just merely exist, but truly live. Don't travel just to be a kid again; define a sense of purpose to your wandering. You can have fun, see all the world that you can, but that in and of itself will leave you feeling unfulfilled. Humans need a sense of purpose, a deeper meaning behind the things we do. For example, if you have a desire to travel and explore unknown places, get to know people as you go. Immerse yourself with them, their culture, lifestyle, and cuisine. Make connections and look for ways you can serve, contribute, or support someone else. If you look for them, there are always opportunities to help others. It may be a piece of advice, a shoulder to cry on, or maybe you help them fulfill a dream. Whatever it may be, there are people who need the kind of help that only you can provide.

This is why finding a mentor or coach is so valuable. It should be a critical part of everyone's life. Yes, you are a powerful human being capable of almost anything you can dream of, but that doesn't mean you will get there alone. In fact, you won't get there alone because everyone needs help.

If you're in a rut, need advice about your marriage, or need to make a change, a coach can help you see a different perspective. When I coach anyone — men, women, or children — I usually point out that it's their choice to commit and believe in order to triumph.

You have the power to change.

You can build the life you want, but I want to remind you to take the pressure of achieving everything right this moment off your shoulders. If you are working on some big goals, they take time. They take effort. They take consistency. They take discipline. Therefore, you need to remember this: you have the power. However, if you put too much pressure on yourself, you may get locked up in indecision. Just take one baby step at a time.

I always remind myself when I start to feel anxious about trying to achieve something, "What's ONE thing that I can accomplish right now in order to move closer to my goals?" Not what are ALL the steps, but just ONE thing that I can do that matters the most right now? Once you have completed that ONE thing, then move on to the next ONE thing.

The ONE thing builds up faster than you think. And it makes the entire process a lot less stressful. Remind yourself this the next time you feel like the pressure is on. It will make your journey more enjoyable and keep you standing in your power. When you're overwhelmed or frustrated, take a break to evaluate your priorities. Your purpose for doing what you do must always be aligned with your goals. Your goals must be aligned with who you are. What is your why? Your why needs to make you cry or else it's not your why. How well can you define your why? Let me give you some tips on defining your why.

What is your purpose?
What is your reason for existence?

If you state that it's just one human in your life, or perhaps an ideal lifestyle, wealth, a specific neighborhood, house, or business, and any of that is taken away from you—what next? Hundreds of fires raged across the western part of the United States, and many have lost their homes, businesses, and even loved ones. This type of debilitating event can be challenging to bounce back from. I know, because when I lost my brother, it was devastating. You can bounce back from any adversity that life throws at you. You were created for a purpose designed just for you here on earth, and it's not dependent on anyone else. Look at Mother Theresa as an example of someone who lived in simplicity and lived a legacy to help orphans. Look around at many other people who are less well known and you can see that even someone with nothing can live such a large life purpose, whether it's your neighbor, the little old lady down the street who lives with intentionality, or a speaker on global stages.

Your purpose is deeper than any human or material thing.

How will you protect it?

If an attacker came at you and your life is at risk, who are you fighting for that would give you Herculean strength to overcome this aggressor? Most of us have experienced the fight-or-flight response. In this example here, flight is not an option. This is a situation where, in order to stay alive, you have to fight with all your might. When you keep in mind who is at home waiting for you and that they would be devastated if something fatal ever happened to you, you will experience "fight mode", an adrenaline rush where you find yourself a hundred times stronger than you thought you could ever be and you will, without a doubt, defeat this attacker.

Who and what motivates you to eagerly want to jump out of bed every day and go slay the dragons that life throws at you? Our why gives us reasons not only to live but to live with a greater purpose and with abundance and fulfillment. Our why gives us a reason to want to make a difference, an impact, to leave a gigantic dent on the universe! Life is not just about me, me, and me. It's bigger than me! Your why should be so big that it directs you to discover solutions to the world's problems, even if you didn't mean to do it! Your why should be the reason for every breath you take.

Always recalibrate: what's your why? Ask yourself this year after year and not just once.

Here's how I discovered my why. When I was a college student, I worked as a nursing assistant at Shriners Hospital for Children, located on campus. I liked my work and had a great experience, but the one thing that I hated most was being told what to do by my bosses. I know that *hate* is a strong word, but it was exactly how I felt back then. As much as I love my husband, I don't even like it when he tells me what to do. He knows better than that. He's welcome to offer up suggestions (not).

My experience at the hospital determined my why for me. That was when I decided that I would pursue a life of entrepreneurship. I am a strong and independent woman who refuses to work under the thumb of others! I will be my own boss, with my own freedom to come and go as I desire! Because my father preferred not to be a slave to others, but he didn't have an option to do differently, he wanted us, his children, to not struggle as he did. My family is my why. My family inspired me to not only dream but to dream big! And to not be afraid to work hard to attain that dream. They are the reason that I push myself every day, to be the best that I can be and to give the most that I can to others.

In order to be true to yourself, you must know who you are.

EXERCISE
9

LIST FIVE SIMPLE RANDOM ACTS OF KINDNESS THAT YOU CAN DO DAILY, IF NOT, THEN WEEKLY.

1. _____

2. _____

3. _____

4. _____

5. _____

List all of your goals. It doesn't matter if they're small, medium, or large. Prioritize them in terms of importance. Start with the most important one. Next to each goal, write down why it's important to you. Finally, for each goal, set and write down a date that you want to accomplish that particular goal. This will help to give you a sense of urgency.

Your date will also help to hold you accountable.

When things are written out and in front of you, you are breathing life into them. They become more real, more relatable, and more attainable!

_____

_____

_____

_____

_____

_____

_____

_____

_____

_____

_____

DR. SUSAN TRUONG

r. Susan Truong is a multilingual award-winning international speaker and optometrist who changes her patients' lives beyond just correcting their sight. She also shares the teaching that how you think can either help or hinder many aspects of your life, both personally and professionally.

Through this priceless gift, she has formed an emotional connection and trust where her patients feel like they matter and feel comfortable opening up to her about their fears, insecurities, and aspirations. This unique rapport with her patients assures them that they are at a safe place with their most intimate stories and where they will not be judged.

Since 2000 when she started her second career as an eye doctor (her first was in medical research where she spent six years), Dr. Susan Truong has impacted so many of her patients' lives, young and old, with her motivational demeanor. Many have gained invaluable insights, along with increased self-worth, confidence, and self-esteem. This, in turn, has given them the much-needed courage to make drastic life changes, such as losing weight, fleeing an abusive/toxic relationship, returning to school years later, leaving an unfulfilling job, climbing out of the dark abyss of depression, kicking an addiction such as drugs, alcohol, smoking, coping with the loss of a loved one or a job; the list goes on.

She respects her patients and recognizes that they are more than a set of eyeballs sitting in her exam chair. She listens with intention and genuinely cares about them and understands that their well-being affects the quality of their life, physically, mentally, emotionally, and spiritually. She teaches that life changes begin with the discipline of practicing a positive and purposeful mindset. With the power of this mindset, unimaginable possibilities and opportunities can and will be unleashed. She inspires her patients to live their lives by finding meaning in the gift of daily living and to not merely exist. She impresses upon everyone the importance of doing their own soul-searching while on the quest to define their purpose, authenticity, and vision.

Besides mastering six languages, Dr. Truong is a serial entrepreneur. After four years of working for other doctors, she started her own practice, which she eventually expanded to five locations with an amazing team of doctors and staff. Being multilingual has helped her to build long-lasting relationships with patients from the Asian and Latin communities.

She is a mentor to pre-optometry students from the University of South Florida and the University of Tampa. They spend time shadowing her in the office and learn what it takes to be a compassionate doctor and the business aspect of the practice as well. She has had a number of her mentees graduate from the Doctor of Optometry program, some from Nova Southeastern University (her alma mater) and others from various optometry schools. She also mentors high-school-age patients as she inquires about their aspirations following graduation. She hopes that sharing her stories of struggles and triumphs helps to inspire these students to pursue their passion.

She has been invited back to Nova Southeastern University several times and to the University of Houston as a guest speaker to share her success stories and business savvy with the upcoming College of Optometry graduates.

She is a faculty member of the Doctor of Healthcare Business program at the University of Berlin, Germany.

As a consultant for Bausch & Lomb and Coopervision, Dr. Truong was the subject matter expert traveling the country, meeting with fellow optometrists and their staff, and sharing her knowledge on various topics such as new products and more effective and ideal methods of delivering optimal care to patients in order to increase business and profitability.

Last, but not least, along with her husband, she is also a real estate investor/developer and the former owner of a booming bar in thriving downtown St. Petersburg, Florida.

She was leading a blessed life, personally and professionally, or at least she thought so, until August 2014 when her world was rocked by the loss of one of her younger brothers to cancer... just nine days after he was diagnosed. His passing posed numerous questions pertaining to the authenticity, vision, and purpose of her own existence. Out of the ashes, the phoenix rose. Out of her darkest and most painful period in her life, she founded "Beyond 20/20 Vision," a forum where she can impact more lives beyond her 6'×10' dimly lit, windowless exam room.

Providing invaluable insights and empowering others to live their vision, to live to their highest self, to live more abundantly and purposefully, to live their authentic life, to control and determine their own destiny by choosing the positive mindset — This is Dr. Susan Truong's passion. This is her greater purpose. This is her vision. This is her legacy.

www.beyondyour2020vision.com
Email: Dr.Susan@beyondyour2020vision.com

MY LOGO

It is unique and precious as intuition. It is beautiful like a gem. The third eye chakra is here represented as a vertical eye in the sublime indigo shade of the deep universe, protected and in elevation on a symbolic open-hands figure. The third eye chakra works on building your inner knowledge, inspiration, and your true purpose. Indigo, which is also known as royal blue, is the color of the third eye chakra. It is the color of deep change. It symbolizes deep inner knowing and wisdom. With the influence of the indigo chakra, you also begin to realize that you can consciously create your life. All it takes for your vision for the future to come true is to employ a creative act of will.

YOUR VISION FOR THE FUTURE

_____

_____

_____

_____

_____

_____

_____

_____

_____

_____

_____

_____

_____

_____

_____

_____

_____

_____

_____

_____

_____

_____

_____

_____

_____

YOUR VISION FOR THE FUTURE

_____

_____

_____

_____

_____

_____

_____

_____

_____

_____

_____

_____

_____

_____

_____

_____

_____

_____

_____

_____

_____

_____

_____

_____

BEYOND20/20VISION

YOUR VISION FOR THE FUTURE

_____

_____

_____

_____

_____

_____

_____

_____

_____

_____

_____

_____

_____

_____

_____

_____

_____

_____

_____

_____

_____

_____

_____

_____